BACKYARD BIRDS OF
Texas

BACKYARD BIRDS OF
Texas

Bill Fenimore

Gibbs Smith, Publisher
TO ENRICH AND INSPIRE HUMANKIND
Salt Lake City | Charleston | Santa Fe | Santa Barbara

To my mentor, Jack Rensel

First Edition
12 11 10 09   5 4 3 2

Text © 2008 Bill Fenimore
Maps © Cornell Lab of Ornithology
Photo Credits: Gary Aspenall: page 34; Randy Chatelain: page 56; Brian L. Currie: page 36; Lee Duer: pages 26, 38; Keith Evans: page 32; Joe Ford: page 18 (inset); George Jett: page 40; Jerry Liguori: pages 22, 28, 44 (inset), 50, 60; Judd Patterson: pages 46, 52 (inset), 54; Tom Pawlesh: pages 20, 42; Dave Rintoul: page 66; Robert R. Ruszala: page 32 (inset); Kelly Thurgood: pages 24, 34 (inset), 44, 52, 58, 62; VIREO: cover, pages 2, 18, 30, 48, 64

Published by
Gibbs Smith, Publisher
P.O. Box 667
Layton, Utah 84041

Orders: 1.800.835.4993
www.gibbs-smith.com

Designed by Rudy Ramos
Printed and bound in Hong Kong

Library of Congress Cataloging-in-Publication Data

Fenimore, Bill.
  Backyard birds of Texas : how to identify and attract the top 25 birds / Bill Fenimore. — 1st ed.
      p. cm.
  ISBN-13: 978-1-4236-0351-1
  ISBN-10: 1-4236-0351-6
  1. Birds—Texas—Identification. 2. Birds—Texas—Pictorial works. I. Title.

QL684.T4F46 2008
598.09764—dc22

2007052701

Contents

Foreword

When I first met Bill Fenimore in 2001, I knew a lifelong friendship was underway. We were about the same age, had grandchildren, and traveled many of the same paths around the world—but that's not what I mean exactly. What struck me most deeply was Bill's infectious enthusiasm for wild birds and his keen desire to share that excitement with others. In many ways, this guide is an inevitable extension of Bill's personality, a natural outlet for his deep appreciation for the satisfactions that come with learning more about wild birds. In this book, Bill has identified those wild birds you will likely see in your own backyard because he knows that your life will never be the same.

In my own work, I often say that the closer we live to each other, the greater we need to live closer to nature. These days, many of us feel the daily pressures of urban or suburban living and yearn for a simpler time when we lived more in tune with natural rhythms and seasonal cycles. We may also feel a tug of desire to live within a smaller framework where we can make a positive contribution to the natural world around us.

In that sense, this guide makes an enormous contribution by revealing new ways to bring more peace and tranquility into our lives by watching and feeding wild birds around our homes.

GEORGE H. PETRIDES SR.
Founder and Chairman
Wild Bird Centers of America, Inc.

Introduction

This guide will enable you to identify and properly name the top twenty-five birds using your backyard bird sanctuary. You will also learn which bird species visit as spring and fall migrants, which are nesting birds, which are winter residents, and which are permanent year-round residents. This guide will educate you about the cover (vegetation), food, and water needs for these birds. It will also show you a variety of ways that you can improve your backyard habitat for birds and the enjoyment you can have watching and caring for them.

Hook Birds

Most birders who develop the enthusiasm that I have can tell you which bird it was that got them hooked. These "hook birds" have been responsible for providing me and others with many years of enjoyment. Some people, like me, get hooked early in life. Others don't feel the hook until much later. I have included here two hook bird stories: mine, which happened when I was a young lad, and that of my brother, who got hooked after retiring from a successful career in the United States Air Force.

Bill's Story

When I was ten years old, I saw a strange-looking bird along the Chester River where I was fishing in southeastern Pennsylvania. I had no idea what it was. At that age, I could have told you what a house sparrow, starling, pigeon, or a robin was, but that was about it. This bird was like none of those familiar birds. It was perched on a log overlooking the river, close to the water surface. Its bill was long and pointed. The bird was motionless, like a statue, poised over the water on its perch. It was watching small minnows swimming ever closer to its position. I noticed it was a slender bird, with blue and green feathers on its back. It had a dark cap with shaggy feathers on the back of its neck. The head and neck were a chestnut color.

Suddenly the bird struck. Its bill pierced the water and it came up with a minnow, neatly held at the tip of its bill. The bird quickly swallowed its catch and with a bold abrasive *kyowk* flew off, soon out of sight, around a bend in the river. I stood there watching in amazement as the bird disappeared. *What was that?* I asked myself.

Later that day I was telling a neighbor who was a local schoolteacher about the strange bird. He went into his house and brought out a book about birds. He instructed me to look through the book and see if I could identify the bird that I had seen along the river. Turning the pages of his field guide, I was impressed with the many beautiful birds that were illustrated on each page. Most of the birds were new to me. They had names that I had never heard before: crossbill, sapsucker, oriole, and so forth. Suddenly, turning the next page, I saw the exact bird I had seen catch the minnow. Excitedly, I pointed it out. "There it is, look," I said. "Why, that's a green heron," the teacher told me. I borrowed the book and studied the green heron's picture the rest of that day. What an amazing bird, I thought. And what an amazing book with all manner of strange birds illustrated in it. That night at the dinner table, I announced to my family that I had seen a green heron while fishing down at the river that day. "What's a green heron?" my father asked me. I pulled out my book and showed him the bird's picture. He stared at it and said, "I've seen this bird before. We always called them mud hens. I never knew their proper name."

I was dumbstruck! As a young fellow, I thought that Dad knew everything. To think that there was something that he didn't know, and that I knew, was a very amazing circumstance. The following day I showed my friends the bird's picture. None of them knew what it was. Well, now I was on to something. I could study this book and learn about birds. Then I could tell my family and friends about them. This was the beginning of my birding hobby, which I have carried on for some fifty-odd years. It has been a very rewarding pastime. It has helped me better identify with nature and appreciate the outdoors.

Brother Len's Story

When I was a kid growing up in Pennsylvania, I only had a mild interest in birds, and that was probably due to my brother's "serious" interest. In those days I remember my brother, Bill, as being the "go-to guy" if you had a question about birds. But my passive interest changed in 1996. Shortly after I retired from the Air Force I joined Bill on a weeklong field trip to Yellowstone National Park. Bill told me in advance to bring along binoculars so that I could better enjoy the wildlife. I expected to see a lot of wildlife. What I didn't expect was to come home with a passion for birding.

On the five-hour drive from Utah to Yellowstone, I noticed that Bill spent more time looking up in the sky than he did looking at the road. "Red-tailed hawk," he would say, spotting a bird soaring high in the sky. Sometimes he would point to a hawk sitting on a telephone pole as we were driving by and say, "Swainson's hawk." His knowledge and skill at being able to identify birds without binoculars (while going sixty miles an hour) impressed me. It wasn't long before he had me doing it. Looking up in the clouds at a bird, I would say, "Red-tailed hawk." Looking at the same bird, Bill would correct me and say, "uh, turkey vulture." *Hmmm,* I would say to myself. *This isn't as easy as it looks.*

We stayed in cabins in Yellowstone's Lamar Valley. Bill quickly befriended another birder. Together they would stop and look at every passing bird and identify it. The excitement and enthusiasm they shared was contagious and I got caught up in the excitement. I would quickly point at a bird flying by that Bill seemed to be ignoring and ask, "What's that?" "Brewer's blackbird," Bill would nonchalantly reply.

After dinner each night we would go out on the porch to watch the wildlife. Under the eaves of the cabin a barn swallow had built a nest. In it were four nestlings. Suddenly an adult flew in, fed each of the begging mouths, and then flew off. Moments later another adult appeared. This went on until dark. To me, it was a magical sight. The next day I saw a mountain bluebird, a beautiful male flying over the field next to our cabin. The bird was the color of the clear blue sky above. I was mesmerized, watching the beauty of the bird as it crisscrossed the field catching insects. At that moment I knew that birding was something I could enjoy.

Since my Yellowstone adventure, my interest in birds has continued to grow. I have traveled extensively across North America and to other countries, learning about birds. I have become an officer in my Audubon chapter, and I even took a Cornell University course on bird biology.

It seems I have found the perfect hobby for my retirement: birding. Thanks, Bill.

Why Feed Backyard Birds?

When I was a toddler, I would watch my mother throw bread crumbs onto the snow of our Pennsylvania yard for the birds. She felt that the birds needed her help weathering cold winter days. It is still a fond memory of mine, some fifty years later. I became fascinated with those birds as I watched them enjoy Mom's treat.

Birds provide a terrific keyhole into the natural world. Once there, you can wade in as deep as you feel comfortable. Some will be content, like Mom, to simply put food out for the birds in winter. Others will want to learn more about the birds, especially about identifying them correctly. Still more will desire to learn how they can help birds, as they enjoy watching them. There are others who enjoy birding so much that they continue the knowledge quest by enrolling in citizen science programs, available through the Audubon Society and the Cornell Lab of Ornithology. Whichever category you fall into, birds are wonderful creatures to enjoy.

What Is Backyard Bird Habitat?

When I was a college student, I read a statement in an American history book that I have never forgotten. It created a powerful and lasting image in my mind. The statement was this: "The forest in northeastern America was so dense when the pilgrims landed at Plymouth Rock that a squirrel could travel from the East Coast to the beginning of the Great Plains without ever touching the ground." Imagine that wonderful expanse of natural habitat for the birds that dwelled there.

Today that expansive and contiguous forest does not exist; such has been the impact of development and spread of our rural, urban, and suburban communities. However, it occurred to me as I began to study birds and their habitat needs that there are many "contiguous backyards" throughout America today. Imagine the positive impact we may have on birds by creating a bird-friendly backyard habitat.

What is habitat? Simply put, habitat is cover, food, and water within a reasonable distance from one another. As birds go about their daily activities, the presence of these three elements is essential. Cover refers to the vegetation that exists in a given area. It provides nesting, roosting, loafing, perching, and shelter areas as well as natural foods. Birds will eat nectar, seed, nuts, acorns, berries, and fruits produced by native and cultivated plantings.

Bird Identification

One of the first things you want to do when determining the identity of a bird is to remember the key physical features of the bird that you observed. You can then consult your backyard bird guide to identify the specific bird you have seen, using those physical features noted as clues. Writing down key physical features always helps me remember them more accurately when later reviewing my guide. The advent of digital cameras makes it easier to take a photograph for later study. Making a simple sketch is also helpful. You can make marks and notes on your sketch that will later help you whittle down the possible suspect list.

Think of yourself as a detective solving a crime. The witness is being asked key questions to help identify the prime suspect. "Was the suspect tall?" you, the detective, ask. "No," the witness answers, "he was short, about five feet." "What was he wearing?" The witness describes his straw hat, red shirt, and brown slacks. "Did he have any scars or tattoos?" And so it goes, until there are sufficient key clues for you, the detective, to positively identify the suspect that you observed.

These questioning techniques will be helpful as you use your backyard bird guide. A helpful first step in bird identification is to note the relative size of the bird you observe. Compare it to the profiled bird scale on the bottom of the page. Move forward or backward in the guide until you are in the correct size range of the bird that you have observed. Profiled birds are the hummingbird (3 3/4 inches), wren (4 3/4 inches), sparrow (6 inches), starling (8 1/2 inches), robin (10 inches), dove (12 inches),

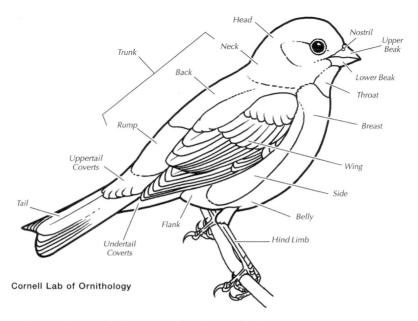

Head
Nostril
Upper Beak
Trunk
Neck
Back
Lower Beak
Throat
Breast
Rump
Uppertail Coverts
Wing
Tail
Side
Flank
Belly
Undertail Coverts
Hind Limb

Cornell Lab of Ornithology

and crow (18 inches). Become familiar with these relative sizes so that you know whether to move forward or backward in the guide.

After noting the relative size of your suspect bird, ask yourself other helpful identification questions. What is the hue of the bird's feathers? Are there any significant identification marks, like the black-and-white-striped crown of a white-crowned sparrow? What is the shape of the bird's mandible (bill or beak)? Is it conical shaped, like that of a house finch? A conical-shaped bill is used for crushing seed and denotes a seed-eating bird. These subtle hints displayed by the bird's physical features will help you narrow the list of suspect birds.

What was the bird doing? Behaviors such as fly catching, drilling into a tree, or eating fruit or nectar are all helpful clues that can separate one bird from another. For example, a robin-size bird eating fruit could be one of the jays, a bluebird, a mockingbird, a waxwing, or a robin. Taking note that this particular bird's feathers were mostly blue eliminates the mockingbird, waxwing, and robin but leaves the jays and bluebirds. The suspect list is getting smaller.

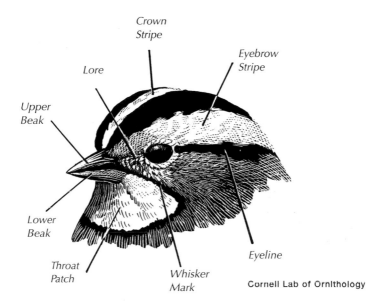

Crown
Stripe

Eyebrow
Stripe

Lore

Upper
Beak

Lower
Beak

Throat
Patch

Whisker
Mark

Eyeline

Cornell Lab of Ornithology

Now check the range distribution map in your bird guide for those remaining suspect birds. The area of the range distribution map where the depicted bird occurs in the nonbreeding season (fall/winter) is colored orange. Summer resident map range distribution areas are colored blue. Green-colored map areas denote permanent year-round residents. This range distribution map will help confirm the presence or absence of the remaining suspect birds: jays and bluebirds. We will use a cold day in February in my native Pennsylvania for our example. The range distribution map for blue jays shows the entire Pennsylvania map colored in green. Aha! Blue jays are permanent residents. The eastern bluebird range distribution range map shows a blue-colored area for the summer. My suspect bird is not likely an eastern bluebird, I begin to think.

Continuing the investigation in our example, I see that the bird at my feeder is eating black oil sunflower seed and it has a crest of feathers raised on its head. Reading the behavior description for the eastern bluebird, I note that it is an insectivore, not a seed eater.

Wing Bars

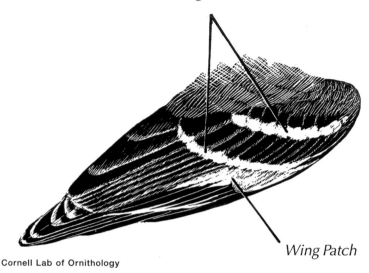

Wing Patch

Cornell Lab of Ornithology

Last but not least, I look at the photographs of both remaining suspect birds, eastern bluebird and blue jay. I can see that the blue jay has a crest of feathers on its head. The eastern bluebird does not show a crest. Now I can confidently see that the bird eating black oil sunflower at my feeder is a blue jay. Its plumage matches the photograph. The crest on my bird is there too. His size is larger than the 7-inch eastern bluebird and the time-of-year range distribution map confirms the blue jay's presence, with the absence of the eastern bluebird in winter.

You will be very pleased to note your progress in being able to sort through the possible suspects until you have determined which visiting bird you are enjoying in your backyard bird sanctuary.

Black-chinned Hummingbird

Archilochus alexandri

DESCRIPTION: The black-chinned hummingbird is a flying jewel that features a violet gorget when flashing on the lower throat. The throat is black when not lit up. The head is a greenish color, with a straight black bill. The upperparts are green. The throat has a white collar just below the gorget. The underparts are whitish with dusky green sides and flanks.

BEHAVIOR: Black-chinned males will defend a breeding territory as they work to attract a mate. Their courtship display is elaborate. The male will fly in a pendulum motion and dive with wings buzzing past the admiring female perched nearby. Hummingbirds will readily use nectar feeders and water misters. Spiders and other insects are eaten, especially when feeding young.

SONG: A twittering *teew-teew-teew.*

HABITAT: Suburban backyard landscapes; lowland and mountain foothills.

NESTING: A tiny nest is built by the female using lichen, as well as plant and tree down bound together with spider silk. The nest is located in the fork of a tree, on a horizontal branch. The nest can stretch with the chick as it grows. One to three white eggs are incubated for 13 to 16 days by the female. Young fledge within 13 to 21 days.

RANGE: Gulf Coast of Texas west to California, and north through the Intermountain West to the Canadian border.

SIZE: $3\,1/2$ to $3\,3/4$ inches.

To Attract: Offer nectar using a ratio of 4:1 water to sugar. Boil water for 2 minutes at a rolling boil, turn off heat, and stir in sugar until it dissolves. Cool and fill feeders. Clean and change nectar every 3 to 4 days so it remains fresh. Hang feeders where they will be shaded most of the day.

Hummingbird	Wren	Sparrow	Starling	Robin	Dove	Crow
$3\,3/4''$	$4\,3/4''$	$6''$	$8\,1/2''$	$10''$	$12''$	$18''$

Ruby-throated Hummingbird

Archilochus colubris

■ Breeding
■ Wintering

DESCRIPTION: The ruby-throated hummingbird is a flying jewel. The male has an iridescent ruby throat called a gorget when it is flashed. The throat looks black when not lit up, contrasting with a white chest and green sides. The tail is black. The bill is long, straight, and black. It has a green crown with green upperparts. The female has green upperparts and white underparts. She has white outer tips on her tail feathers.

BEHAVIOR: The ruby throated humingbird feeds on the nectar from wildflowers, which it helps pollinate. It will also take insects and spiders, particularly when feeding young, as a source of protein. It will rob insects from spiderwebs and hawk insects in flight. It will also take sap from sapsucker wells and insects trapped in the sap. Males fly a pendulum display flight that forms a 180-degree arc.

SONG: Rapid chatter; twitter notes.

HABITAT: Suburban landscapes, parks, and gardens; fields with wildflowers.

NESTING: The female builds a small cup nest from soft plant material, thistle down, and lichen, bound together with spider webbing. The nest is just large enough to contain the jellybean-size eggs. Two white eggs are incubated for 11 to 16 days by the female. Altricial young (born naked, eyes closed, and helpless) fledge within 22 days.

RANGE: Throughout the eastern United States and west to the Mississippi River.

SIZE: $3\,^3/_4$ inches with a wingspan of $4\,^1/_4$ to $4\,^1/_2$ inches.

> **To Attract:** Offer nectar made from water and sugar (4:1 ratio of water to sugar). Do not use red food dye. Boil water 2 minutes at a rolling boil. Turn off heat. Slowly pour sugar into the hot water while stirring until sugar dissolves and goes into solution. Cool. Make more than you need and store extra in refrigerator. Change nectar every 3 to 4 days so that it remains fresh. Specialty nature stores offer a convenient liquid nectar or quick-dissolving powder. Plant flowers and vines with tube- or bell-shaped blossoms.

Hummingbird	Wren	Sparrow	Starling	Robin	Dove	Crow
$3\,^3/_4$''	$4\,^3/_4$''	6''	$8\,^1/_2$''	10''	12''	18''

Carolina Chickadee

Poecile carolinensis

DESCRIPTION: The Carolina chickadee has a black cap and bib with white cheeks. The upperparts are gray with gray edging on the forward part of the wing. Underparts are white with buffy gray on flanks. It has a short, dartlike, pointed black bill. The tail is short and shows a slight notch in it. Both sexes are similarly plumaged.

BEHAVIOR: The Carolina chickadee is a regular visitor to backyard habitats with trees and woody shrubs. It is found in pairs during the breeding season. It will form mixed flocks with downy woodpeckers, juncos, kinglets, nuthatches, titmice, and other small songbirds in winter.

Suet and sunflower seed feeders are good attractors. Chickadees will also glean insects, spiders, moths, and caterpillars from foliage. They will eat small berries when available.

SONG: Four-note *see-bee-see-bay* whistled quickly with the first and third notes high pitched. The *chick-a-dee-dee-dee* call is used as a warning signal, with the increased number of *dees* at the end indicating the presence and type of danger.

HABITAT: Deciduous forests with clearings; edges and backyard suburban areas.

NESTING: The chickadee is a cavity nester that will readily use a nest box. Make the entrance hole opening $1^1/_8$ to $1^1/_2$ inches in size. Place 1 to 2 inches of wood chips on the bottom of the nest box.

RANGE: South of an irregular boundary that slices through southern New Jersey and Pennsylvania, and bisects Ohio, Indiana, Illinois, Missouri, and southern Kansas.

SIZE: $4^3/_4$ inches with a wingspan of $7^1/_2$ inches.

 **To Attract:** Erect a convertible nest box that chickadees can use for nesting. The nest box, which can be found in specialty nature stores, includes a viewing panel and, later, a winter roost. Mount it on a tree trunk at Grandpa's hoisting height (the height that you can hold up a grandchild to look into it).

Hummingbird	Wren	Sparrow	Starling	Robin	Dove	Crow
$3^3/_4''$	$4^3/_4''$	6''	$8^1/_2''$	10''	12''	18''

American Goldfinch

Carduelis tristis

■ **Breeding**
■ **Year-round**
■ **Nonbreeding**

DESCRIPTION: The American goldfinch is the beautiful yellow "canary" of backyard habitats. Adult male breeding plumage is a bright yellow, set off by black wings with white wing bars and a black cap. The female is grayish brown with an all-yellow head.

Many backyard observers do not recognize the winter goldfinch when it loses its bright yellow breeding plumage. It molts into a rather drab grayish or brownish plumage so that its energy can go into maintaining its body rather than its bright feathers during winter.

BEHAVIOR: The goldfinch is a flocking bird in winter that gathers around backyard feeders and habitats. It feeds on seed-producing flowers, like dandelion and weed seeds. A shallow water feature where it can bathe and drink is a welcome mat for the goldfinch.

SONG: The goldfinch is very vocal, especially in flight where its call note is likened to the mnemonic "po-tato-chip" or "per-chick-oree, perchickoree."

HABITAT: Open areas with trees and shrubs. Backyards provide ideal habitats. Easily attracted to feeders and water features.

NESTING: The nest is woven plant material with plant down, especially from the thistle. The goldfinch incorporates spider silk and caterpillar webbing in its nest construction. Four to six bluish-white eggs are incubated by the female for 10 to 12 days. Fledging takes place within 11 to 17 days. It has one or two broods per year. Both parents feed the young.

RANGE: Throughout the continental United States.

SIZE: 5 inches with a wingspan of 8 to 9 inches.

 **To Attract:** Use Nyjer and black oil sunflower seed. Nyjer seed in a sock or tube feeder is an ideal way to attract these colorful songbirds.

Hummingbird	Wren	Sparrow	Starling	Robin	Dove	Crow
3¾''	4¾''	6''	8½''	10''	12''	18''

White-breasted Nuthatch

Sitta carolinensis

■ Year-round

DESCRIPTION: The white-breasted nuthatch has an all-white face and chest. A black crown extends down the back of the neck. The long black bill turns up slightly at the tip. The underparts are white with a rusty tinge on the flanks. The upperparts are blue-gray with blackish-blue wings with white edging.

BEHAVIOR: The nuthatch displays a unique foraging behavior. It flies to the top of a tree and works its way down to the bottom, circling branches and the tree trunk as it descends head first. It eats insects, spiders, tree nuts, and seeds. It will roost in tree cavities in winter. It is sociable in winter when it joins mixed foraging flocks.

SONG: A nasal sounding *yank-yank, yank* and an ascending *wahwahwah-wahwah.*

HABITAT: Deciduous forests; woodlots; suburban landscapes with trees.

NESTING: This is a cavity nester that will use a nest box. Both parents build the nest in a cavity using shredded bark, feathers, and hair. Three to ten whitish pink eggs with reddish brown freckles are incubated by the female for 12 days. Altricial young (born naked, eyes closed, and helpless) fledge within 14 days.

RANGE: Across the continental United States in suitable habitat.

SIZE: 5 to 6 inches with a wingspan of 9 to 11 inches.

 **To Attract:** Erect a convertible nest box with a predator guard, found in specialty nature stores. Orient entrance hole in an easterly direction for morning sun.

Hummingbird	Wren	Sparrow	Starling	Robin	Dove	Crow
3³/₄''	4³/₄''	6''	8¹/₂''	10''	12''	18''

Carolina Wren

Thryothorus ludovicianus

■ **Year-round**

DESCRIPTION: The Carolina wren features a bold white stripe above its eye, set off by the reddish brown of its head feathers. The back and upperparts are a rich rusty brown. The wings and tail show bars of darker brown. The mandible is long and has a slight downward curve. The chin, throat, and breast are white. The lower underparts are tawny brown.

BEHAVIOR: Carolina wrens remain in pair groups throughout the year and mate for life. They frequent thickets and are more often heard than seen. However, making squeaky "pishing" sounds will often bring out these curious birds. The tail is held up over the back as the bird probes and digs for insects, caterpillars, larvae, vertebrates, and berries.

SONG: The mnemonic for the song of the Carolina wren is "tea kettle, tea kettle, tea kettle." Only the male sings, and he is very vocal, singing from an exposed perch. Neighboring males may often have singing duels from the large repertoire of more than thirty songs.

HABITAT: Woodlots, farms, and suburban yards in and around deciduous trees and woody shrubs.

NESTING: The wren is a cavity nester that will use a nest box. The female incubates four to eight white to light pink eggs. Altricial young (born naked, eyes closed, and helpless) fledge within 14 days. Both parents will feed the young.

RANGE: Eastern Kansas north into southern Ontario, across to Massachusetts, southward to the Gulf Coast, and into northeastern Mexico.

SIZE: 5 to 6 inches with a wingspan of 11 inches.

To Attract: Erect a nest box. Offer mealworms and suet.

Hummingbird	Wren	Sparrow	Starling	Robin	Dove	Crow
3¾"	4¾"	6"	8½"	10"	12"	18"

Chipping Sparrow

Spizella passerina

■ **Breeding**
■ **Year-round**
■ **Wintering**

DESCRIPTION: The distinctive chestnut cap set off by the long white eyebrow and black eye line distinguishes this sparrow in its summer breeding plumage from other sparrows. The bill is black and the cheeks, nape, and chest are gray. The upperparts are light brown with black or brown steaks and two white wing bars. The tail is long and slightly notched.

BEHAVIOR: The chipping sparrow is usually solitary or in pairs during breeding season. It joins winter flocks of mixed species during foraging forays around woodland edges and thickets. Chipping sparrows eat caterpillars, insects, spiders, and seeds.

SONG: Rapid, repetitive series of *chip* notes, given in a trill on a level pitch. It also uses a thin *ssip* or *seek* call.

HABITAT: Suburban backyards, gardens, lawns, hedges, and grassy fields; coniferous and deciduous forest edges.

NESTING: The chipping sparrow nests often in hedges, thick vine tangles, or branches. The female builds a nest and uses weed stalks, grass, hair, and soft plant material. Two to five greenish-blue eggs wreathed with brown, blue, and black marks are incubated 11 to 14 days. Altricial young (born naked, eyes closed, and helpless) fledge within 8 to 12 days and are fed by both parents.

RANGE: Widespread throughout most of the continental United States.

SIZE: $5\frac{1}{2}$ inches with a wingspan of 8 to 9 inches.

To Attract: Offer proso millet on a platform feeder found in specialty nature stores.

Hummingbird $3\frac{3}{4}$'' Wren $4\frac{3}{4}$'' Sparrow 6'' Starling $8\frac{1}{2}$'' Robin 10'' Dove 12'' Crow 18''

House Finch

Carpodacus mexicanus

■ **Year-round**

DESCRIPTION: The male house finch has a red forehead. The red wraps around the side of its head over the eyes. The throat and chest are red. The top of the head is brown. The upperparts have brown streaks, and the wings display two narrow white wing bars. The chest and underparts have brown streaks. Occasionally the red on males is tinged with orange or yellow. Females and juveniles are dull brown overall with streaking on the breast and sides.

BEHAVIOR: A gregarious flocking bird in winter, the house finch is one of the more widely distributed backyard birds. It was originally from the West and was accidentally introduced to the East in New York in the early 1940s. During winter it will form mixed flocks, particularly with the American goldfinch and pine siskin.

SONG: A three-note rising warble ending with a very high, sharp note. Call notes are *chirps*.

HABITAT: Urban and suburban backyards; parks, gardens, and open woodlands; desert and wooded canyons.

NESTING: The female builds a nest in trees, shrubs, dense bushes, nest boxes, vines, and under building eaves, using grass, twigs, feathers, and other material. Two to six light blue eggs with black and purplish spots are incubated by the female for 12 to 14 days. Altricial young (born naked, eyes closed, and helpless) fledge within 19 days.

RANGE: Throughout the continental United States.

SIZE: 6 inches with a wingspan of $9\frac{3}{4}$ inches.

 **To Attract:** Offer black oil sunflower in tube or hopper feeders available at specialty nature stores.

Hummingbird	Wren	Sparrow	Starling	Robin	Dove	Crow
$3\frac{3}{4}$''	$4\frac{3}{4}$''	6''	$8\frac{1}{2}$''	10''	12''	18''

House Sparrow
Passer domesticus

■ **>31 birds/route**
□ **1–31 birds/route**
□ **<1 bird/route**

DESCRIPTION: The male house sparrow displays a black bib with a gray crown and cheeks. The upperparts include a chestnut nape bordered with a white stripe and a white wing bar. The back is buffy brown with black streaks. The underparts are gray. The female has a pale buffy eyebrow line and a plain gray chest with a striped black and brown back.

BEHAVIOR: The house sparrow hops along the ground as it forages. It gathers in flocks in winter. The sparrow is a loud, gregarious bird. It eats insects, seeds, grain, and spiders. It will glean insects from tires and grilles of automobiles in parking lots.

SONG: *Chirps* and repeated *cheeps.*

HABITAT: The house sparrow is the bird of the city. It has adapted well to urban landscapes after being introduced in New York City in the 1850s.

NESTING: Both parents build the nest, which is a rough hodgepodge of grasses, weeds, debris, twigs, and feathers. The nest is located in building crevices, nest boxes, vine tangles, and other sheltered areas. Three to seven green or blue eggs with gray and brown spots are incubated by both parents for 10 to 14 days. Altricial young (born naked, eyes closed, and helpless) fledge within 17 days.

RANGE: Across the continental United States and into Canada and Mexico.

SIZE: 6 inches with a wingspan of $9\,^1/_2$ to 10 inches.

 **To Attract:** Offer proso millet on platform or hopper feeders.

Hummingbird	Wren	Sparrow	Starling	Robin	Dove	Crow
$3^3/_4$''	$4^3/_4$''	6''	$8^1/_2$''	10''	12''	18''

Downy Woodpecker

Picoides pubescens

■ **Year-round**

DESCRIPTION: The downy woodpecker is the smallest woodpecker. Black and white overall, the male has a red nape. The back is white, bordered by black wings, with white spotting on the wings. The face has a black stripe through the eye and a black malar mark. The bill is short, stubby, and half the length of the head (back to front). There are black crosshatch markings on the outer tail feathers (not easily seen). The underparts are white.

BEHAVIOR: Downy woodpeckers forage in trees for insects and insect egg larvae. They will readily come to suet feeders. When establishing breeding territories, they drum on dead branches and other resonating objects to attract a mate and designate territory boundaries.

SONG: A short *pik* or *chik* call and a soft, high-pitched whinny.

HABITAT: All tree areas, especially suburban backyards.

NESTING: A cavity nester, it will excavate its own cavity and will use a nest box.

RANGE: Found throughout all but the southwestern United States.

SIZE: 6 1/2 inches with a wingspan of 11 to 12 inches.

To Attract: Hang suet feeders and a good, formulated, nonmelting suet available at specialty nature stores. Erect a nest box sized for the downy woodpecker with an entrance hole of 1 1/4 to 1 1/2 inches.

Hummingbird	Wren	Sparrow	Starling	Robin	Dove	Crow
3³/₄"	4³/₄"	6"	8¹/₂"	10"	12"	18"

Tufted Titmouse

Baeolophus bicolor

■ **Year-round**

DESCRIPTION: The upperparts of the tufted titmouse are gray with a tuft that can be raised and flattened on the head. The bill is straight, short, and black. The underparts are white with rusty flanks. Feet and legs are gray-black.

BEHAVIOR: The titmouse is an active bird that forages in the trees for insects, insect larvae, spiders, seeds, berries, tree nuts, and acorns. It will cache seeds and nuts in the crevices of bark. It forms mixed foraging flocks with downy woodpeckers, juncos, kinglets, nuthatches, and other small songbirds in winter. The titmouse will take a nut or seed to a favorite branch, place it between its feet, and pound it open with its bill like a jackhammer.

SONG: *Peeto-peeto-peeto* whistled in a series. Call note is *see-nyahh* in a scolding tone.

HABITAT: Woodlands, parks, and suburban landscapes.

NESTING: The titmouse is a cavity nester. The female builds the nest with leaves, grass, moss, snakeskin, mammal fur, and hair. Four to eight white eggs with brown freckles are incubated by the female for 13 to 14 days. Altricial young (born naked, eyes closed, and helpless) fledge within 18 days.

RANGE: From the Gulf Coast states up to New England.

SIZE: $6\frac{1}{2}$ inches with a wingspan of $10\frac{3}{4}$ inches.

To Attract: Erect a nest box with the entrance hole facing an easterly direction for morning sun.

Hummingbird	Wren	Sparrow	Starling	Robin	Dove	Crow
$3\frac{3}{4}''$	$4\frac{3}{4}''$	$6''$	$8\frac{1}{2}''$	$10''$	$12''$	$18''$

White-throated Sparrow

Zonotrichia albicollis

■ **Breeding**
■ **Year-round**
■ **Wintering**

DESCRIPTION: The white-throated sparrow has a distinctive white bib. It has crown stripes that are black or brown, with a similar eye line. The mandible is dark, and there are yellow lore spots in front of the eye. The back is a rusty brown with two white wing bars. The underparts are gray with light streaking on the flanks.

BEHAVIOR: The white-throated sparrow is primarily a ground feeder that gathers in mixed-species flocks in winter and individually or in pairs during the breeding season. It hops along, occasionally scratching among the leaf litter for seed and insects. If it is hidden in the underbrush or thicket, a visual response can usually be elicited with squeaky "pishing" sounds.

SONG: The mnemonics are "oh sweet Kimberly, Kimberly, Kimberly" or "poor Sam Peabody, Peabody, Peabody." Call note is a sharp *tseep.*

HABITAT: Thickets; weedy fields; shrubs, ground cover, and hedgerows; urban and suburban yards and gardens.

NESTING: The female builds a nest using grass, twigs, pine needles, moss, and softer plant materials for a liner. The female incubates three to six white and blue-green eggs. Altricial young (born naked, eyes closed, and helpless) fledge within 12 days and are fed by both parents.

RANGE: Northern states into Canada; during winter, from the Mid-Atlantic states to the Gulf Coast states.

SIZE: $6\,^3/_4$ inches with a wingspan of 10 inches.

To Attract: Scatter white proso millet, black oil sunflower, or cracked corn on a platform feeder near ground cover.

Hummingbird	Wren	Sparrow	Starling	Robin	Dove	Crow
$3^3/_4$''	$4^3/_4$''	6''	$8^1/_2$''	10''	12''	18''

Eastern Bluebird

Sialia sialis

DESCRIPTION: As their name implies, bluebirds are predominantly blue on the upperparts. The throat and chest are a robinlike reddish brown, and the belly is white. The female has a paler color pattern than the male. Juvenile bluebirds begin to show traces of blue on the tail and wings. They have a spotted breast, reminiscent of young robin fledglings.

BEHAVIOR: Bluebirds are insectivores that hawk insects in open meadows, woodlands, fields, and park areas. Perching on a branch or overhead telephone wire, bluebirds will fly down to catch insects in grassy fields below. They will also eat spiders, frogs, earthworms, and berries.

SONG: A warbling *chur chur-lee chur-lee*. The call note is *true-lee*.

HABITAT: Open expanses in meadows, parks, open woodlands, fields, and large backyards in suburban areas.

NESTING: Bluebirds are cavity nesters. They were in decline because of habitat loss from increased development as well as competition for cavities from non-native European starlings. However, they have rebounded with the erection of nest boxes made for bluebirds. Entrance holes of $1\,9/_{16}$ inches are recommended to allow bluebirds entrance while restricting starlings. Approved Bluebird Society nest boxes are available at specialty nature stores. Several bluebirds will keep warm overnight in winter by roosting and huddling together in nest boxes. Two to seven light blue eggs are incubated for 12 to 14 days by the female. Altricial young (born naked, eyes closed, and helpless) fledge within 20 days.

RANGE: Primarily from the East Coast to the Midwest into southern Canada and eastern Mexico.

SIZE: 7 inches with a wingspan of $11\,1/_{2}$ to 13 inches.

 **To Attract:** Use a nest box with a properly sized entrance hole. Offer mealworms to attract bluebirds. The combination of nest boxes and mealworms will attract bluebirds in suitable habitat areas.

Hummingbird	Wren	Sparrow	Starling	Robin	Dove	Crow
3³/₄''	4³/₄''	6''	8¹/₂''	10''	12''	18''

Brown-headed Cowbird

Molothrus ater

DESCRIPTION: The male has a brown head and a glossy black body with a small conical-shaped bill. The female is plain grayish brown with a faint streaking on the underparts. Juveniles are streaked on the underparts until molting.

BEHAVIOR: The brown-headed cowbird is a parasitic bird that deposits its eggs in the nests of other birds. It will often remove the host's eggs to make room for its own egg. This is a strategy developed from following roaming herds of bison, a practice that did not allow time for nest building, incubation, and brooding chicks. Some small songbird reproduction success is jeopardized by cowbird nest parasitism. Cowbirds have expanded their range as humans develop land and clear forests.

Cowbirds gather in large flocks after the breeding season and will join other blackbird flocks in winter. They forage on the ground while walking with their tail held up, particularly near domestic livestock.

SONG: Low and long gurgle call notes and high, thin notes in flight.

HABITAT: Open meadows and fields; pasture areas with cattle.

NESTING: The female will lay one light blue egg with brown flecks in another bird's nest; she can lay 10 to 36 eggs in various songbird nests in a single season. Eggs hatch before host eggs in 10 to 13 days. Young cowbirds will usually outcompete the host chicks.

RANGE: Throughout the continental United States and into Canada and Mexico.

SIZE: 7 to $8\frac{1}{4}$ inches with a wingspan of $11\frac{3}{4}$ to $13\frac{3}{4}$ inches long.

To Attract: Erect hopper-style and platform feeders with small seeds, such as proso millet, cracked corn, and black oil sunflower seed.

Hummingbird	Wren	Sparrow	Starling	Robin	Dove	Crow
$3\frac{3}{4}$''	$4\frac{3}{4}$''	6''	$8\frac{1}{2}$''	10''	12''	18''

Great Crested Flycatcher

Myiarchus crinitus

■ **Breeding**
■ **Year-round**
■ **Wintering**

DESCRIPTION: This bird has a crest that when raised gives the head a bushy appearance. The head and back are olive brown. The throat and chest are gray, which sets off the contrasting yellow belly. The tail and wings are rusty brown, most evident in flight.

BEHAVIOR: The great crested flycatcher likes to sit high in the canopy of a tree, usually on a dead branch that gives it good visibility for nearby flying insects. It will sally forth hawking an insect, often returning to the same perch. During the spring breeding season, males can be seen chasing females in courtship flights.

SONG: A sharp, whistled *wheep* followed by a long *berg* or *prrrrreeet*.

HABITAT: Large tracts of parks and suburban yards with tall trees.

NESTING: The great crested flycatcher is a cavity nester that can be attracted to a nest box placed high on a tree trunk or under a building eave. The female incubates four to eight creamy white eggs. Altricial young (born naked, eyes closed, and helpless) fledge within 21 days and are fed by both parents.

RANGE: Gulf Coast states north to Canada, and from the East Coast to the Midwest.

SIZE: 7 $\frac{1}{2}$ inches with a wingspan of 12 to 14 inches.

 **To Attract:** Erect a nest box 6 to 15 feet high on a tree trunk in a quiet part of the yard. Orient the hole facing east so that it gets sun in the morning but not all day long.

Hummingbird	Wren	Sparrow	Starling	Robin	Dove	Crow
3¾''	4¾''	6''	8½''	10''	12''	18''

Purple Martin

Progne subis

■ Breeding

DESCRIPTION: The purple martin is the largest of the swallows. The male is a dark, iridescent blue-black. The tail is forked. Females have blue-gray upperparts and gray-white underparts.

BEHAVIOR: Colonial flocks feed on insects caught on the wing, with occasional foraging for insects on the ground.

SONG: A chirpy, gurgling series of notes given in flight and in the predawn.

HABITAT: Open meadows, clearings, parks, and open suburban areas. Likes to use condo-style purple martin nesting houses with multiple apartments.

NESTING: The purple martin is a colonial cavity nester in the eastern United States, while western birds are solitary nesters in tree cavities. Both sexes bring leaves, feathers, and grasses to the nest. Three to eight white eggs are incubated by the female. The altricial young (born naked, eyes closed, and helpless) fledge within 31 days. The young are fed by both parents.

RANGE: Throughout the east and Midwest; more casual in the west. Winters in South America.

SIZE: 8 inches with a wingspan of 16 inches.

 **To Attract:** Erect a purple martin house that will attract a colony of purple martins. The colony will act as an effective natural control of insects.

Hummingbird	Wren	Sparrow	Starling	Robin	Dove	Crow
3¾''	4¾''	6''	8½''	10''	12''	18''

European Starling

Sturnus vulgaris

■ Year-round
■ Nonbreeding

DESCRIPTION: The European starling is black overall. The feathers in breeding plumage have a green-purple sheen. The body shape is chunky with a very short tail. The European starling walks rather than hops. Its long, thin, pointed bill is yellow in spring and off-white to gray in winter. White spots cover its body in winter plumage. Juveniles are dull gray.

BEHAVIOR: This is a flocking bird in winter that can gather in the tens of thousands. The starling is a very gregarious, urbanized bird that has adapted well to the city, town, and countryside. It is non-native to the United States, introduced in New York in 1890. Its diet is extremely varied, including insects, mixed grains, and fruit.

SONG: A variety of whistles, gurgles, clatters, and twitters.

HABITAT: Urban and suburban landscapes.

NESTING: Starlings will nest in natural cavities, nest boxes, buildings, and other structural crevices, such as backyard grills, competing with native species. They will evict woodpeckers from cavities that they have constructed. Nest material is a wide variety of plant material, assembled in a random and shabby fashion. Four to eight blue-green eggs are incubated for 12 to 14 days by both parents. Altricial young (born naked, eyes closed, and helpless) fledge within 18 days. It has two to three broods per year.

RANGE: Throughout the continental United States and Canada. The starling is likely the most prolific and abundant bird on the continent.

SIZE: $8^1/_2$ inches with a wingspan of $15^1/_2$ inches.

To Attract: Set out suet and seed feeders and erect nest boxes.

Hummingbird	Wren	Sparrow	Starling	Robin	Dove	Crow
$3^3/_4$''	$4^3/_4$''	6''	$8^1/_2$''	10''	12''	18''

Northern Cardinal

Cardinalis cardinalis

DESCRIPTION: The male northern cardinal is striking bright red with a red crest and a black mask around the eyes and on the throat under the bill. The bill is conical shaped and red. The female is duller olive brown on the upperparts with a buffy golden head with a crest and a large conical-shaped pink bill. The underparts are buffy brown and the wings show a red wash. Juveniles resemble females but with a black bill.

BEHAVIOR: Northern cardinals are found in pairs during breeding season. They form mixed foraging flocks in winter. They prefer trees and shrub edges with dense, low cover. Cardinals frequent parks, suburban backyards, and marshes and forests. They will eat insects, seed, fruit, and grain.

SONG: A loud song that includes whistles and gurgles, including the mnemonic "what-cheer, what-cheer." Call note is a *tchip*.

HABITAT: Woodlands and forest edges; farmland; parks and suburban backyards with shrubs, trees, and thickets of low cover; marshes.

NESTING: The female builds a nest of grass, bark, twigs, and other plant material, lined with hair and grass in a shrub or tree. Three to four pale greenish or bluish eggs with gray, brown, or purple spots are incubated 12 to 13 days by both parents, primarily the female. Altricial young (born naked, eyes closed, and helpless) fledge within 11 days.

RANGE: East Coast to the Midwest and down into the Gulf Coast states and Mexico.

SIZE: 7 1/2 to 9 inches with a wingspan of 12 inches.

 **To Attract:** Offer black oil sunflower seed in a hopper feeder.

Hummingbird	Wren	Sparrow	Starling	Robin	Dove	Crow
3 3/4"	4 3/4"	6"	8 1/2"	10"	12"	18"

Red-bellied Woodpecker

Melanerpes carolinus

■ **Year-round**

DESCRIPTION: The red-bellied woodpecker has black and white barring down the back. It has a red crown and nape with a pale buffy chest and face. The red belly for which it is named is not always seen but is low on its belly and between the legs when visible.

BEHAVIOR: This is a very vocal woodpecker that drums in the spring to establish a breeding territory. Red-bellied woodpeckers eat insects, seeds, suet, berries and fruits, and sap taken from sapsucker wells.

SONG: Loud repeated *churr,* and *chuck, chuck.*

HABITAT: Forests and forest edges; swamps; parks and suburban landscapes with trees.

NESTING: Both sexes excavate a cavity-nesting chamber. Three to eight white eggs are incubated by both parents for 11 to 14 days. Young fledge within 27 days.

RANGE: Northern and southeastern United States into the Midwest.

SIZE: $9^1/_2$ inches with a wingspan of 15 to 18 inches.

 **To Attract:** Offer suet, shelled tree nuts and peanuts, and hulled sunflower seeds.

Hummingbird	Wren	Sparrow	Starling	Robin	Dove	Crow
3³/₄''	4³/₄''	6''	8¹/₂''	10''	12''	18''

American Robin

Turdus migratorius

■ Breeding
■ Year-round
■ Nonbreeding

DESCRIPTION: Perhaps the most recognized backyard bird in North America, the American robin is widely distributed throughout the continental United States. Although thought of as a harbinger of spring, the robin is found throughout the year in most of its range. It will migrate south of the snow line in winter when snow exceeds four inches in depth.

The robin features a brick-red breast. It has a yellow bill with a broken white eye ring. The throat is white with black striping. The back is gray. Juveniles when first fledging from the nest have a spotted chest and underparts; otherwise they resemble adults.

BEHAVIOR: Spring finds males fighting and defending territories that are made up of various neighborhood yards. Males will often fight their shadows in low windows in spring. They are often seen probing the yard for earthworms and other invertebrates. Robins switch to a fruit and berry diet in winter when worms are not available. Solitary or in pairs in spring, robins gather in large winter communal flocks.

SONG: A very vocal singer, often into the night with its repeated "cheerily cheer-up cheerio" phrase. Vocalizations vary with a whinny and sharp warning *tut-tut-tut*.

HABITAT: Urban/suburban lawns and yards with trees and shrubs.

NESTING: The robin builds a classic round grass nest with a mud bottom located in the fork of a tree. It will also use a nesting shelf. Robins usually locate their first nest in a conifer (it already has its leaves in early spring). A second nest and brood is raised in a deciduous tree that has leafed out by early summer. Occasionally, a third brood is raised. Three to seven sky-blue eggs are incubated by the female for 12 to 14 days. The altricial young (born naked, eyes closed, and helpless) fledge within 14 to 16 days.

RANGE: Throughout the continental United States.

SIZE: 10 inches with a wingspan of 14 to 16 inches.

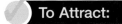 **To Attract:** Plant fruit- and berry-producing shrubs and trees that robins can use in spring and winter, such as mulberry, crabapple, pyracantha, and mountain ash. Robins will use suet if it is presented so that they can perch to reach it.

Hummingbird	Wren	Sparrow	Starling	Robin	Dove	Crow
3¾''	4¾''	6''	8½''	10''	12''	18''

Northern Mockingbird

Mimus polyglottos

■ Year-round

DESCRIPTION: The northern mockingbird is an overall gray bird with two white wing bars that become large white wing patches when seen in flight. The tail is long and has white outer tail feathers.

BEHAVIOR: The northern mockingbird is a fairly common bird in its range that forages in and around shrubs, trees, and edges of gardens and backyards. It eats insects, fruit, and berries. It vigorously defends its nesting area, attacking any animal, bird, or person passing nearby. It is often seen running on the ground and flashing its wings to flush insects.

SONG: The mockingbird is a mimic that sings and imitates other sounds and birdsongs. It sings repetitive phrases with a loud *tchack* call.

Mockingbirds will often sing all night during breeding season.

HABITAT: Suburban landscapes; parks, gardens, and farms. Well adapted to living in backyard habitats.

NESTING: Both parents build a nest in a shrub or tree with a variety of sticks, twigs, leaves, and string, lined with softer plant materials. Two to six bluish-green eggs spotted with brown are incubated by the female for 12 to 13 days. Altricial young (born naked, eyes closed, and helpless) fledge within 13 days.

RANGE: Eastern and southwestern United States into California.

SIZE: 10 inches with a wingspan of 13 to 15 inches.

 To Attract: Offer suet and dried fruits. Plant trees, shrubs, and vines that will produce persistent crops of berries and fruit.

Hummingbird	Wren	Sparrow	Starling	Robin	Dove	Crow
3¾''	4¾''	6''	8½''	10''	12''	18''

Blue Jay

Cyanocitta cristata

■ **Year-round**

DESCRIPTION: Blue jays are very bright, flashy, and vocal birds. They have a crest that can be raised or lowered. The face and throat bib are grayish white with the neck adorned by a black necklace. The blue wings show a white wing bar. The blue jay has gray-white underparts and a blue back. Both sexes are similar in plumage characteristics.

BEHAVIOR: Blue jays have adapted to urban/suburban backyards and parks. They are very intelligent birds and are extending their range. They are most often found in pairs during nesting season and can be found in gregarious flocks in late summer. Blue jays are vocal birds who warn other birds when a predator, such as a cat, hawk, or owl, is present.

They are omnivorous but a large portion of their daily intake is acorns, seeds from pinecones, corn, fruit, and berries. They are opportunistic and will take eggs or nestlings. Carrion, insects, mice, meadow voles, other small mammals, small snakes, frogs, and small amphibians are included in a varied diet.

SONG: A loud *jayyy* and a *wheedle, wheedle*. It can mimic other birds, especially hawks.

HABITAT: Parks, backyards, and suburban landscapes with oak and beech hardwood trees.

NESTING: Both parents build a nest of twigs, grass, lichen, and other soft plant matter in the crotch of a tree. Three to seven pale greenish-blue eggs with dark brown marks are incubated by both parents for 16 to 18 days. Altricial young (born naked, eyes closed, and helpless) fledge within 17 to 21 days.

RANGE: Throughout the Northeast and Midwest where large canopy oak and beech hardwoods exist. Range is extending into the Northwest.

SIZE: 11 inches with a 16-inch wingspan.

To Attract: Offer black oil sunflower seed in a hopper feeder. Blue jays will use suet and take peanuts in or out of the shell. A water feature with a heating element will provide a bathing area that they will use regularly.

Hummingbird	Wren	Sparrow	Starling	Robin	Dove	Crow
3¾''	4¾''	6''	8½''	10''	12''	18''

Mourning Dove

Zenaida macroura

■ Breeding
■ Year-round
■ Nonbreeding

DESCRIPTION: The mourning dove is a brownish-gray bird with black spots on the upper wing. Male doves show a pinkish tinge on the breast and a black spot on the cheek with a blue-gray crown. The tail is long and all of the tail feathers are tipped in white on the ends. The female is a faded brown. Juveniles have a scaled appearance.

BEHAVIOR: Males will aggressively defend breeding territories. Doves will form flocks after the breeding season. They feed on a variety of seeds and grains. Their wings make a whistling sound during takeoff.

SONG: A mournful coo repeated *cooo, cooo, cooo, cooo* by the male in breeding season.

HABITAT: Fields and agricultural areas; parks, gardens, and suburban backyards.

NESTING: The female pulls together a loose assortment of twigs that makes a flimsy platform in a tree or shrub. Two white eggs are incubated by both parents for 14 days. Altricial young (born naked, eyes closed, and helpless) fledge within 14 days. The young squab is fed crop milk, which is produced in the crop and regurgitated with seeds. Several broods are raised during the breeding season.

RANGE: Throughout the continental United States and into Canada and Mexico.

SIZE: 12 inches with a wingspan of 17 to 19 inches.

 **To Attract:** Offer black oil sunflower seed, cracked corn, or proso millet on a platform feeder.

Hummingbird 3³/₄'' Wren 4³/₄'' Sparrow 6'' Starling 8¹/₂'' Robin 10'' Dove 12'' Crow 18''

Common Grackle

Quiscalus quiscula

DESCRIPTION: Note the overall glossy black body with a purple iridescent sheen on the back. There is also a bronze-colored type whose back has a bronze contrast with the blue-black head. The eyes are a pale white-yellow; the bill is long, strong, and sharply pointed. The tail is long and has a crease down the middle, giving it a wedged shape.

BEHAVIOR: The grackle is common east of the Rocky Mountains, particularly in cities, suburban communities, agricultural areas, woodlands, and marsh wetlands. Grackles walk on the ground. The common grackle is a gregarious bird that gathers in large flocks in winter. They will nest in groups and forage together. Their diet is diverse and varied, including insects, caterpillars, spiders, worms, seed, crop grains, fruit, small mammals, eggs and nestlings, grubs, invertebrates, and small fish.

SONG: A sound like a rusty hinge creaking open with a gurgling added to it. A hard *chuk* note is also used.

HABITAT: Suburban backyards and parks; open areas and forest edges; farms and pasture lands; marsh wetlands.

NESTING: The female builds a bulky nest that includes twigs, grass, mud, feathers, and other debris that is lined with softer plant material and fibers. Four to seven light brown or green eggs with brown and lilac markings are incubated by the female for 13 to 14 days. Altricial young (born naked, eyes closed, and helpless) are fed by both parents and fledge within 20 days.

RANGE: Throughout the continental United States; especially common east of the Rocky Mountains and north into Canada.

SIZE: 11 to 13 $^1/_2$ inches with a wingspan of 17 to 18 $^1/_2$ inches.

To Attract: Use hopper or platform feeders with cracked corn, proso millet, and black oil sunflower seed.

Hummingbird	Wren	Sparrow	Starling	Robin	Dove	Crow
3³/₄''	4³/₄''	6''	8¹/₂''	10''	12''	18''

Northern Flicker (Yellow-shafted)

Colaptes auratus

DESCRIPTION: The northern flicker is a large woodpecker with underwing colorations that differ based on its geographical distribution. The "yellow-shafted" form occurs from northern Canada into the Midwest, down into the Gulf states, and north throughout the East and New England. The "red-shafted" form occurs in the western United States. When it is in flight, the flicker shows the flashing yellow or red underwing. The flicker also has a rounded white rump patch shown in flight on top of its back where the tail joins the body. The bill is a long and stout chisel.

The male red-shafted flicker has a red mustache. The male yellow-shafted flicker has a black mustache and a red crescent on the back of the neck. Both forms have a gray-brown crown, face, and nape. The upperparts are brown with black barring. The underparts show a prominent black bib with scattered large dark spots on a white chest and belly. Females lack the mustache.

BEHAVIOR: Flickers are most often seen on the ground, where they forage for ants. When ants are not available in winter, they frequent backyards with suet. Flickers drum in spring to establish breeding territories.

SONG: A loud and bold *wick-er, wick-er* note repeated and a sharp *kleeyah* note for the call.

HABITAT: Forests, parks, gardens, and suburban backyard landscapes.

NESTING: Both parents excavate the cavity that can be in a dead snag, pole, or a nest box. Three to twelve white eggs are incubated by both parents for 11 to 16 days. Altricial young (born naked, eyes closed, and helpless) fledge within 28 days.

RANGE: Across Canada and the continental United States into Mexico, distribution varying by form.

SIZE: $12^{3}/_{4}$ to 14 inches with a wingspan of 19 to 21 inches.

To Attract: Offer suet on a tail prop suet feeder and peanut splits in a peanut feeder found at specialty nature stores.

Hummingbird	Wren	Sparrow	Starling	Robin	Dove	Crow
$3^{3}/_{4}''$	$4^{3}/_{4}''$	6''	$8^{1}/_{2}''$	10''	12''	18''

FEEDING PREFERENCES
OF FAVORITE BACKYARD BIRDS

Birds

Food Types

Perching Birds

1. Bluebirds
2. Cardinal, Northern
3. Chickadees
4. Finch, House
5. Finch, Purple
6. Goldfinches
7. Grosbeaks
8. Hummingbirds
9. Jays
10. Nuthatches
11. Orioles
12. Siskin, Pine
13. Titmouse, Tufted
14. Woodpeckers
15. Wren, Carolina

Ground Feeding Birds

16. Dove, Mourning
17. Juncos
18. Sparrow, House
19. Sparrows, Native
20. Towhees

Food Types:
- Oil Sunflower
- Hulled Sunflower
- Striped Sunflower
- Millet
- Nyjer (Thistle)
- Cracked Corn
- In-shell Peanuts
- Shelled Peanuts
- Suet
- Safflower
- Mealworms
- Fruit
- Nectar

■ = Most Preferred
▨ = Preferred

MEALWORMS

Safflower

Millet

Pure Beauty Suet

Tropical Sunflower

Black Oil Sunflower

Reference Materials

Supplemental feeding

Some backyard birds are ground-feeding birds. Native sparrows, such as the dark-eyed junco, towhee, dove, quail, and pheasant, naturally feed on the ground (i.e., a flat surface). Others are considered perching birds, such as the colorful American goldfinch, house finch, and black-capped chickadee. These birds like to feed from a perching position.

Understanding a bird's preferred feeding style and behavior guides us toward the proper style of bird feeder selection. A platform feeder is an imitation of the ground that sparrows, doves, and quail will readily use. Scattering the right seeds on it, since these birds are seed eaters, will provide an attraction that they will soon come to enjoy—seed on a flat surface. A tube feeder with perches will attract perching birds: finches, chickadees, and goldfinches.

Positioning feeders at different height levels—hanging from tree limbs, on the ground, and in intermediate height areas—will provide birds with varying space dimensions that mimic natural feeding and foraging behavior. Place feeders where they can be easily watched and enjoyed as you observe the birds attracted to your backyard bird sanctuary. A nectar feeder placed in a flower bed around a patio area can provide delightful entertainment as you watch hummingbirds and orioles visiting the flowers for their nectar, as well as your sugar water.

Remember that there are more species of birds than just seed-eating birds. Provide sugar water in nectar feeders. There are a variety of feeder styles available that will enable you to present a wide assortment of food for the birds visiting your backyard bird sanctuary. There are feeders made to present mealworms, suet, fresh or dried fruit, jelly, tree nuts, and peanuts, in addition to a wide assortment of seeds. This variety of feeders and food assortment will help you attract a wide variety of birds.

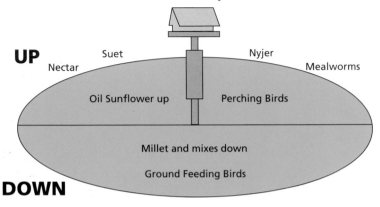

What Do I Feed Birds?
Where Do I Put My Feeder?

UP
Suet
Nectar
Nyjer
Mealworms
Oil Sunflower up
Perching Birds
Millet and mixes down
Ground Feeding Birds
DOWN

The Rule: Sunflower up. Millet Down.

The Question: Where do you want to watch birds from?

Warblers, vireos, and bluebirds will come readily to feeders offering mealworms. Woodpeckers and other insect-eating birds will be attracted to suet. Chickadees, finches, and siskins are just a few of the birds that will come to seed feeders. Orioles, robins, and mockingbirds are readily attracted to fruit, berries, and jelly.

Attracting and Understanding Hummingbirds

The hummingbird is a marvel of nature. You will never forget the first time you see one of these flying jewels visiting your backyard bird sanctuary.

Hummingbirds are attracted to and return to feeders that contain nectar resembling flower nectar. This nectar can be made at home with four parts boiling water to one part table sugar. Dissolve sugar in water and allow to cool to room temperature. Store for up to four weeks in a clean sealed jar in your refrigerator. Hummingbirds like fresh nectar, so only place enough nectar in your feeder that will be consumed in three days. Nectar sours in about four days when over 80 degrees F. Do not use red dye, honey, juice, fructose, artificial sweetener, brown sugar, or syrup in hummingbird nectar. These are dangerous to hummingbirds.

Nectar-producing flowers are very attractive to hummingbirds. Some of these that you may plant include the following: trumpet vine, columbine, honeysuckle vine, red penstemon, cardinal flower, bleeding hearts, bee balm, fuchsia, coral bells, and scarlet sage.

East of the Mississippi River there is only one type of hummingbird, the ruby-throated hummingbird. West of the Mississippi River there are several species, depending on your location and suitable habitat: Allen's, Anna's, black-chinned, broad-tailed, calliope, Costa's, and the rufous hummingbird. The rufous hummingbird is copperlike in color. The male is a big bully at the feeder. The black-chinned male has a dark, almost black head and throat. The broad-tailed male has a green head and garnet throat. The calliope is the smallest hummingbird in North America. The male has a garnet-streaked throat with a green head.

Mealworms for Birds

Mealworms can entice a bird to use a nearby nest box. They help an incubating female find food quickly, so her eggs are not left for long periods of time. Mealworms provide protein for nestlings, and they help birds survive during spells of severe winter weather, when food is hard to find. They are clean, easy to care for, do not carry human diseases, and are readily accepted by birds.

Keep mealworms in a refrigerator. Do not allow them to freeze; take them out every five to seven days. Allow them to warm up and start moving around (takes about one to two hours). Place cubes of apple $1/4$ inch in size in with them and leave for another one to two hours. Refrigerate again. Remove old apple cubes when you take them out for the next warming-and-feeding period and replace with new apple cubes.

In your backyard, place the mealworm feeder in the open, clearly within a bird's view. Place the feeder near existing feeding areas so that the birds will be able to easily find the new treat. Many birds are attracted to mealworms, including the chickadee, oriole, black-headed grosbeak, robin, cedar waxwing, jay, woodpecker, house wren, house finch, and goldfinch.

Protecting Birds from Cats and Other Predators

Place feeders where they are not within an easy leap of an ambush spot. I like to place ground feeders at least two cat bounds away from any cover. This provides the feeding birds an opportunity to detect and escape the cat. Cats are not native to this country. Birds have not evolved with domesticated cats, so they do not readily recognize them as dangerous.

Another method I use to provide added safety for the birds coming to my backyard bird sanctuary is to place a short garden fence with a large wire grid around the bird feeding area. The large grid opening in the fencing allows the birds to come and go easily. The short fence is easy for me to step over when refilling feeders. However, it is a barrier that the charging cat must navigate. This provides the birds with more opportunity to elude the cat.

Keeping a cat inside the house is the very best way to keep and enjoy a cat. They live longer lives when kept inside, avoiding accidents with vehicles and harassment from other critters, and they can safely enjoy watching birds through the window.

Bird Baths and the Importance of Water

A bird bath is perhaps the easiest way to provide the greatest diversity of bird species visiting the backyard. Many migrating birds will stop to

bathe and drink. Resident birds will soon learn of reliable local water features. They will visit the bath regularly.

When birds learn of a reliable open water source in winter, when all other water is frozen solid, they will "flock" to your backyard bird sanctuary. You will be delighted with the diversity and number of birds visiting your water feature. My wife called me recently one cold winter day to show me the twenty-five American robins using our bird bath. There were several more perched nearby, awaiting their turn at the "bird spa." You can keep your bird bath water from freezing with a heating element. If you are planning to purchase a bird bath, look for styles that incorporate a heating element that is controlled with an internal thermostat. If you already own a bird bath, you can buy a heating element that is designed for use in a bird bath. It is a good investment. The birds will be the benefactors. You will be too, just as Mom and I were as we enjoyed watching our visiting birds.

Regular bathing is important for the birds. They must bathe, clean, and preen their feathers to keep themselves aerodynamically fit. Clean feathers are better insulators that enable the bird to trap air. The air is heated by the body, which keeps the bird warm during those cold winter days and nights.

Water in a bath should have a depth ranging between $1/2$ inch and $1^1/2$ inches. Any deeper is of little use to birds. Birds prefer water at ground level, so the higher off the ground the bath, the less birds will use it. Fresh, clean water is attractive to birds, not dirty, algae-filled water. The more natural the water feature looks, the more birds will use it.

Remember:

Standing water is good
Dripping water is better
Misting water is great
Moving water is best

Birds are especially vulnerable while bathing. Wet feathers will slow their take-off and flight considerably. Therefore, birds are very cautious while bathing. Provide a safe bathing site for them and they will use it. A bath out in the open without any cover nearby (two to four feet away) makes a bathing bird vulnerable to attack from a bird of prey.

Pishing

Pishing is an onomatopoeic squeak, squeal, or stuttering slur emitted by a birder to lure a bird hidden from view into the open. Everyone is familiar with the famous saying: "A bird in hand is worth two in the bush." A birder would say "a bird in view in the bush is all I desire."

Often you catch a blur of movement in the yard as a bird flits into the cover of a nearby hedge or shrub. Some birds are natural skulkers, fox sparrows and catbirds, for example.

You wait but it will not come into view. The mystery bird is quiet, so there is no song to identify. You are not quite sure what bird it is. Yet you crave a view to satisfy your quest to know and identify it. Hence, you rely on your ability to pish, i.e., coax the bird out of the cover and into view.

Many birds will respond to alarm or mobbing calls out of curiosity. Chickadees, wrens, and nuthatches are particularly piqued by pishing. I use four types of pishing:

The first is a low sounding *pish-pish-pish,* as I force air against my lips with clenched teeth. The air pushes my lips open to make the pishing sound. Slow and low pishing in groups of three notes is usually sufficient.

My second style is a louder, more rapid series *pish-pish-pish,* with teeth slightly apart and lips closed. The force of air pushes my lips open, as if giving a kiss.

The third manner is to kiss the back of my hand while sucking air into my mouth. The loud squeak is repeated.

Sparrows respond best to a loud and sharp *chip* note. Hold your middle and index fingers against closed lips and give a high-pitched kiss. Repeat this kiss chip sound at one-second intervals for four or five notes.

Once you have lured the bird into view for identification, stop pishing. Don't overuse pishing, since you do not want to tax the birds or distract them from their daily routine.

Cover

Cover is the vegetation that exists in your yard that creates suitable habitat for birds. A key use of cover is for nesting. Besides feeding and bathing, birds need to have a safe place where they can make a nest and raise their young. Nesting cover can be shrubs, trees, vines, and other similar growth that gives the birds a structure to build a nest where they can safely lay eggs, incubate, and fledge their young. Some birds are ground nesters, such as pheasants and quail. Other birds build a nest off the ground, such as the robin and oriole.

Then there are the cavity nesters. Cavity nesters such as the woodpecker can drill and excavate a cavity in a tree. They will make a new cavity each year. Creating a cavity is part of the bonding ritual that the birds go through. Males show potential mates that they can acquire and defend a breeding territory. They will attract a female to their territory by showing existing cavities. The female visits and decides whether she will nest there. It is usually the female who builds and constructs the actual nest. Other cavity nesters will use old woodpecker holes or natural cavities. Some will excavate their cavities like the woodpecker. You can also erect a nest box to simulate the cavity. Erecting a nest box will give you the opportunity to provide suitable habitat for these interesting birds.

Nest Box Building

Nest boxes serve as a replacement of the natural cavity that cavity-nesting birds seek out. Placing nest boxes in suitable habitat enables cavity nesters to raise their young. The nest box also gives us an opportunity to enjoy the birds during this critical time in their lives.

Which bird will live in a particular nest box is determined primarily by the size of the entrance hole. Beyond that, there are recommended interior dimensions for the various species that make up the cavity-nesting birds. The following list includes some of the birds who are cavity nesters: chickadee; northern flicker; downy and hairy woodpecker; Williamson's and red-naped sapsucker; white-breasted, red-breasted, and pygmy nuthatch; juniper titmouse; western screech owl; house wren; eastern, mountain, and western bluebird; starling; house sparrow; tree swallow; American kestrel; and wood duck.

Remember that a nesting bird wants its nest to be secluded, out of the hustle and bustle of other birds, animals, and people. Don't locate your nest box next to your bird feeder or birdbath. Do not place a perch below the entrance hole, or other birds will use it to harass and worry the birds inside. A mother bird may abandon a nest if she is stressed in such a manner.

A nest box needs to be cleaned out in the fall after each nesting season. More than two broods may be raised within a season, so wait until fall to clean it out. Hang the nest box so that it gets morning sun. Place the entrance hole facing northeast, east, or southeast. The entrance hole should not receive afternoon sun. Place clean wood shavings or chips in chickadee and nuthatch nest boxes. Woodpecker boxes can be filled with shavings or chips so that they can "excavate" the box. This method prevents European starlings from entering a nest box.

Most boxes can be hung at "Grandpa's hoisting height." This is the height that I can lift up my grandkids so that they can see what is happening in the box without my needing to climb up a ladder with them in tow.

One particularly enjoyable nest box to place in your backyard bird sanctuary is the convertible nest box. It is a uniquely designed nest box that can be used by birds year-round. The nest box entrance hole located on the front panel of the nest box can be swiveled back and forth from the top (up) to the bottom (down) of the nest box depending on the season of the year. During spring the nest box entrance hole is placed in the top (up) position. The ventilation holes located high up on the side panels are placed in the open position. A small mesh wire platform is placed inside on the floor of the nest box. Hot air rises. This configuration facilitates free air flow through the nest box. There is a Plexiglas side panel that can be opened to inspect activity inside the nest box. You will delight when you open this panel and see a nest with eggs or young nestlings inside. After the nesting season is over in the fall, you reverse the entrance hole to the bottom (down) position on the front of the nest box. Next you close the vents on the inside panels and remove the old nest. It is important to remove the old nest from the nest box. It makes the nest box ready for new nest construction the following spring. Building a new nest is part of the bonding ritual of the breeding birds using the nest box.

Now the nest box is snug and ready for winter. There are two peg perches on the inside of the box that are raised up off the floor above the entrance hole that is now at the bottom of the nest box. These will serve as perches for winter roosting birds. Cold air sinks. Roosting birds perched on the two pegs will have their body heat trapped in the upper chamber of the nest box (remember that hot air rises). This arrangement will keep them warm and protected from the cold of long winter nights. The entrance hole has a metal strip around the outside edge so that squirrels or raccoons cannot chew the hole to make it wider, thus preventing them from gaining access to the eggs or young nestlings. There is an additional predator guard in place, as the entrance hole is two thicknesses of the faceplate board on the nest box. This prevents a raccoon from reaching his paw inside to grab the eggs or young nestlings.

Vegetation for Backyard Birds
Trees Used Primarily for Food

Abies sp. (fir)
> brown creeper, cedar waxwing, chickadee, finch, flycatcher, junco, kinglet, mourning dove, nuthatch, robin, western scrub and Steller's jay

Acer sp. (maple)
> American goldfinch, cedar waxwing, finch, grosbeak, pine siskin, robin, sparrow, vireo, warbler

Alnus italica (Italian alder)
> American goldfinch, chickadee, finch, mourning dove

Betula nigra (river birch)
American goldfinch, chickadee,
finch, mourning dove

Carpinus betulus 'Fastiagata'
(European hornbeam)
American goldfinch, finch,
grosbeak

Celtis sinensis (hackberry)
cedar waxwing, mockingbird,
oriole, robin, thrasher, thrush,
titmouse, towhee

Celtus australis (nettle)
cedar waxwing, mockingbird,
oriole, robin, thrasher, thrush,
titmouse, towhee

Crataegus sp. (hawthorn)
blue, western scrub, and Steller's
jays; cedar waxwing, flicker,
oriole, pine siskin, robin,
thrush, towhee

Ficus sp. (fig)
flicker, grosbeak, oriole, robin,
warbler

Fraxinus sp. (ash)
cedar waxwing, chickadee, finch,
grosbeak, pine siskin, robin,
western scrub and Steller's jay

Juglans sp. (walnut)
flicker, oriole, sparrow, warbler,
western scrub and Steller's jay,
woodpecker

Liquidambar styraciflua (sweetgum)
American goldfinch, chickadee,
finch, mourning dove, pine
siskin, sparrow, towhee,
woodpecker

Magnolia sp. (magnolia)
robin, thrush, vireo

Malus sp. (crabapple)
American goldfinch, cedar
waxwing, finch, flicker, oriole,
robin, towhee, warbler, western
scrub jay, woodpecker

Quercus sp. (oak)
flicker, oriole, mourning dove,
towhee, western scrub and
Steller's jay, woodpecker

Picea sp. (spruce)
American goldfinch, cedar waxwing, chickadee, finch, mourning dove, pine siskin, sparrow, woodpecker

Prunus sp. (cherry, plum)
American goldfinch, cedar waxwing, finch, flicker, grosbeak, oriole, robin, sparrow, thrush, towhee, vireo, western scrub jay, woodpecker

Prunus caroliniana (Carolina cherry)
American goldfinch, cedar waxwing, finch, flicker, grosbeak, oriole, robin, sparrow, thrush, towhee, vireo, western scrub jay, woodpecker

Prunus ilicifolia (holly leaf cherry)
American goldfinch, cedar waxwing, finch, flicker, grosbeak, oriole, robin, sparrow, thrush, towhee, vireo, western scrub jay, woodpecker

Prunus lusitanica (Portuguese laurel)
American goldfinch, cedar waxwing, finch, flicker, grosbeak, oriole, robin, sparrow, thrush, towhee, vireo, western scrub jay, woodpecker

Rhus lancea (African sumac)
California quail

Schinus mollis (California pepper)
cedar waxwing, flicker, robin, thrush

Umbellaria californica (California bay)
Steller's jay, Townsend's solitaire

Shrubs Used Primarily for Food
Arbutus unedo (strawberry tree)
American robin, cedar waxwing, western scrub jay

Arctostaphylos sp. (manzanita)
American robin, fox sparrow, western scrub jay

Arctostaphylos uva-ursi (bearberry)
American robin, cedar waxwing, sparrow, thrush, warbler

Elaeagnus sp. (Russian olive)
cedar waxwing, finch, flicker,

grosbeak, oriole, robin, sparrow, thrush, towhee, vireo, warbler, woodpecker

Heteromeles arbutifolia (toyon)
California quail

Ilex sp. (holly)
cedar waxwing, chickadee, finch, flicker, mourning dove, nuthatch, robin, thrush, towhee, vireo, warbler, western scrub jay, woodpecker

Ligustrum (privet)
cedar waxwing, finch, sparrow, towhee, wren

Mahonia sp. (Oregon grape)
cedar waxwing, mockingbird, robin, sparrow, towhee

Myrica californica (Pacific wax myrtle)
chickadee, flicker, towhee, warbler

Pyracantha sp. (firethorn)
cedar waxwing, flicker, nuthatch, robin, sparrow,

thrush, towhee, vireo, western scrub jay, woodpecker

Rhamnus californica (coffeeberry)
cedar waxwing, oriole, robin, thrush, warbler, western scrub jay

Rhus ovata (sugar bush)
California quail

Ribes sp. (gooseberry)
finch, flicker, robin, thrush, towhee, western scrub jay

Ribes californica; Rosa californica
(California gooseberry; California wild rose)
California quail, grosbeak, junco, pheasant, sparrow, Townsend's solitaire

Rubus sp. (blackberry, bramble)
cedar waxwing, finch, grosbeak, mourning dove, robin, sparrow, thrush, towhee, vireo, warbler, western scrub jay

Sambucus sp. (elderberry)
California quail, cedar waxwing,

finch, flicker, grosbeak, mourning dove, nuthatch, robin, sparrow, Steller's jay, thrush, towhee, vireo, warbler, western scrub jay, woodpecker

Symphoricarpos sp. (snowberry)
    cedar waxwing, grosbeak, robin, thrush, towhee

Vaccinium sp. (huckleberry)
    California quail, chickadee, flicker, grouse, robin, Swainson's thrush, waxwings

Viburnum sp. (honeysuckle)
    cedar waxwing, grosbeak, robin, sparrow, starling, thrush, towhee

Vitis sp. (grape)
    cedar waxwing, finch, mourning dove, robin, sparrow, thrush, western scrub jay

Grasses to Enhance Wild Bird Habitat

Ornamental grasses, especially native types, attract many birds. They are used for nesting materials, nesting sites, and seeds for food. There are many beautiful grasses to select from. Some of the birds that are attracted to grasses include meadowlarks, quail, sparrows, and finches. Here are just a few of the grasses that seem to be especially favored:

Andropogon sp. (bluestem)
Arrhenatherum elatius var. *bulbosum* (tall oatgrass)
Bouteloua gracilis (blue grama)
Briza sp. (quaking grass)
Cortedaria selloana (pampas grass)
Deschampsia sp. (tufted hair grass)
Elymus sp. (wild rye)
Festuca sp. (fescue)
Miscanthus sp. (maidenhair grass)
Muhlenbergia rigens (deergrass)
Panicum sp. (witchgrass)
Stipa sp. (needlegrass)

Annuals and Perennials Used for Food

Amaranthus sp. (amaranth)
Aquilegia sp. (columbine)
Aster
Calendula officinales (pot marigold)

Campanula sp. (bellflower)
Celosia sp. (cockscomb)
Centaurea cyanus (garden cornflower)
Chrysanthemum
Cirsium sp. (thistle)
Coreopsis sp. (tickseed)
Cosmos
Echinacea
Helianthus sp. (sunflower)
Limonium sp. (statice)
Myosotis (forget-me-not)
Nigella sp. (love-in-a-mist)
Papaver sp. (poppy)
Phlox sp.
Portulaca sp. (moss rose)
Rudbeckia sp. (black-eyed Susan)
Scabiosa sp. (pincushion)
Sedum spectabile (ice plant)
Solidago sp. (goldenrod)
Tagetes (marigold)
Verbena sp.
Zinnia sp.

Nectar-producing Plants to Attract Hummingbirds

Trees

Aesculus sp. (horse chestnut)
Alibizia julibrissin (silktree)

x *Chitalpa tashkentensis* (chitalpa)
Citrus
Crataegus sp. (hawthorn)
Melaleuca sp.

Shrubs

Abelia
Arctostaphylos sp. (manzanita)
Buddleia sp. (butterfly bush)
Chaenomeles sp. (flowering quince)
Correa sp. (Australian fuschia)
Diplacus sp. (monkey flower)
Feijoa sallowiana (pineapple guava)
Galvezia speciosa (Bush Island snapdragon)
Grevellia sp.
Heteromeles arbutifolia (toyon)
Hibiscus syriacus (rose of Sharon)
Lavandula sp. (lavender)
Jasminum sp. (jasmine)
Kolwitzia sp. (beauty bush)
Lantana
Ribes sp. (gooseberry)
Rosmarinus sp. (rosemary)
Trichostema (bluecurls)
Vitex agnus-castus (chaste tree)
Weigelia
Yucca sp.

Perennials/Annuals

Aguilegia sp. (columbine)
Agave sp.
Ajuga (bugleweed)
Alce sp.
Alstroemeria (Peruvian lily)
Althea sp. (hollyhock)
Antirrhinum (snapdragon)
Asclepias tuberosa (butterfly weed)
Castilleja sp. (Indian paintbrush)
Dahlia
Delphinium
Dianthus
Digitalis purpurea (foxglove)
Echium fastuosum (pride of
   madeira)
Fuschia
Gladiolus
Hemerocallis (daylily)
Heuchera
Impatiens balsamina (balsam)
Ipomopsis
Iris
Kniphofia (red hot poker)
Lilium
Lobelia cardinalis (cardinalflower)
Lupinus (lupine)

Marabilis
Monarda didyma (scarlet beebalm)
Nicotiana
Oenothera
Pelargonium
Penstemon (beard tongue)
Petunia
Phaseolus coccineus (scarlet runner
   bean)
Phygelius (cape fuschia)
Salvia sp. (sage)
Saponaria (soapwort)
Tropaeolum sp. (nasturtium)
Verbena
Zauschneria sp. (California fuschia)
Zinnia

Vines

Campsis radicans (trumpet vine)
Cestrum elegans (red cestrum)
Distictis buccinatoria (blood red
   trumpet vine)
Ipomoea
Lonicera (honeysuckle)
Tecomaria capensis (cape honey-
   suckle)

Creating a Safe Experience for Birds Visiting Your Feeder
—David J. Horn, Director of Research, Wild Bird Centers of America

In 1999, thousands of American crows died with the arrival of West Nile virus in New York City. The virus quickly spread, reaching the West Coast in 2003. As the virus spread from coast to coast, tens of thousands of birds died including hawks, jays, and chickadees. Fortunately for people who feed birds, West Nile virus is not known to be transmitted from bird to feeder to bird contact; rather, the predominant mode of transmission is from mosquito to bird.

There are, however, several diseases that birds can acquire at feeding stations if they are not properly cared for, and it is important for people who feed birds to create a backyard environment that is safe for our feathered friends. Follow the described steps recommended by the National Wildlife Health Center (www.nwhc.usgs.gov) to reduce the risk of disease to birds using your feeders.

First, provide birds with a large amount of space for feeding. Birds crowded onto a single feeder increase the likelihood of contact between sick and healthy birds and may increase a bird's stress level while feeding, making them more susceptible to disease. One solution would be to purchase feeders that minimize contact between birds. Overcrowding at feeders may also be alleviated by providing birds with other places to feed.

A second step is to keep the birds' feeding area free of a buildup of seed hulls and bird droppings by cleaning the area below the feeder. One way to minimize the cleaning needed would be to use no-waste seeds or seed mixes that contain hulled seeds, and to offer only the preferred seeds for the bird species in your area.

Third, purchase feeders that do not have sharp points or edges. Such feeders may cause bleeding or scratches on birds that can result in the transmission of disease.

Regularly cleaning your feeders is the fourth step you can take. Feeders should be washed approximately once a month with a solution of 10 percent bleach (one part bleach to nine parts water) by completely immersing feeders for at least three minutes and then allowing them to dry. Purchasing feeders that are made of materials that are easier to clean, such as metal and plastic, may also make cleaning the feeder easier.

Finally, store food appropriately and ensure that fresh seed is in your feeder. Use a rodent-proof container to store food, and avoid having wet, moldy, musty-smelling seed in your feeder. Providing feeders that protect the seed from the elements and placing seeds that birds in your area prefer should reduce the chance of seed getting wet or moldy.

In addition to the above steps, people who provide water to birds should scrub their bird bath and change the water in their bath several times per week to prevent mosquito reproduction and the possible spread of West Nile virus.

Bird feeding is a wonderful pastime and it provides those who feed birds with a greater connection to the natural world we live in. Providing a safe and clean feeding environment will allow you to enjoy our feathered friends while lowering the risk to birds of disease at feeders.

To learn more about additional ways to improve the bird feeding experience, download a copy of the 6 steps to turn your yard into a sanctuary for birds brochure on the Wild Bird Centers of America Web site (http://www.wildbirdcenter.com/cms/www_files/6ways.pdf)

Fun Bird Projects

A fun project for the individual or family is to keep a backyard bird list. Each time a new bird species arrives in my backyard bird sanctuary, I record it on my "backyard bird list." Over the last twenty-one years that I have lived in our present home I have recorded new birds visiting the backyard bird sanctuary. The list stands today at eighty-seven different bird species.

Over that same time period, I have continued to make improvements to the habitat. Trees that I planted twenty-one years ago have become substantial cover assets for the birds today. Nearly all of my plantings produce a crop of some sort. It might be crabapples, berries, grapes, acorns, or blossoms that produce. They also provide a harbor for insects, their larvae, and cocoons. The birds will enjoy foraging among the cover to discover what might be there for them to eat.

Nesting, loafing, and roosting cover is available for them too. There are several water features from the traditional pedestal bath to a mister, water dripper, and recycling pump that keep the water moving. The water dripper performs two functions: it moves water and replaces water lost through evaporation or splashing of bathing birds. Included in the water features are several rocks that I have placed to create structure and differing depth levels. Some birds like the robins will jump right into the deep end of the bath. Others like the American goldfinch like the shallow end of the bath. Chickadees like to pick up drops of water coming from the dripper. The pedestal bath is allowed to overflow into a ground-level bath below it, so that the doves, quail, and other ground-feeding birds can access the water. Present water and food at the level that mimics the bird's natural behavior. Doing so will reward you with birds flocking to your backyard bird sanctuary.

Additionally, I keep a list of when the different bird species arrive in my backyard bird sanctuary. This helps me to be prepared for those migratory species that I may only see for a short period of time. Lazuli buntings arrive in my backyard by April 1. I make sure that the platform feeder has ample white proso millet for them. April 15 brings a smile to my face while many others may be fretting and grimacing over their tax return. The hummingbirds are back. Nectar feeders are cleaned and hung with fresh nectar. May 1 will bring orioles. The mealworms, grape jelly, and orange halves are out and waiting for them. The red hot poker flowers are beginning to bloom. I have hung a ball of wool and cotton for nesting material that the oriole will pick at when making its basket-shaped nest in our cottonwood. The Bullock's oriole will find everything ready and the table set for his arrival. June is nesting and fledging time. Robins will be bringing their young onto the lawn where they will hunt worms. Young quail are following their mom through the scrub oak. They can leave the nest and begin following mom and foraging a few hours after hatching. July is a time for young to grow and stretch their wings. Some of the birds begin to molt. Goldfinches are late nesters and are bringing newly fledged young to the Nyjer feeders filled with those tiny black seeds bursting with oil. August and September begin to show early migration in some of the birds. Orioles will soon depart, as well as the hummingbirds. The Neotropical birds put on an extra layer of fat at my feeders in preparation for the migration that will take them far to the south, some as far as Central and South America. October arrives and I clean out the nest boxes so that they will be ready for use as winter roosting areas. The entrance hole is moved from the top of the box to the bottom. The air vents are closed and the old nest removed. Suet is placed in the feeders for the flickers and ruby-crowned kinglets that will winter in my yard. House finches eagerly take the black oil sunflower seeds I place in my tube or hopper-style feeders.

The spotted towhee arrives with winter's first snowstorm in November. His migration is one of elevation. Deepening snow higher up on the mountain forces this ground feeder down into sheltered valleys. My backyard is an ideal wintering area for him. My brush pile, low-growing shrubs, and Oregon grapevine tangle are ready to provide him the cover he desires, as well as areas to scratch about for seeds. Seed has been scattered under the brush pile for him to find. White-crowned sparrows arrive with the towhees. Dark-eyed juncos arrive soon after the towhees. Downy woodpeckers and black-capped chickadees form mixed foraging flocks with these sparrows. Together they will winter in the brush piles, hedges, shrubs, and thickets in the backyard. December shows that winter is here in earnest. Snow is deepening in the yard. I have shoveled a path around to the feeders from my garden shed where I store my seed in galvanized cans. Bright orange pyracantha berries are attracting cedar waxwings to the backyard sanctuary now. The grandchildren press their noses against the cold of the glass window as they watch the birds at the feeders. Quail and pheasant tracks are in my shoveled pathway. They use it so they can avoid slogging through the deeper snow. January is announced by the hooting of a great horned owl. A few nights later I hear the whinny of a screech owl. The owl breeding season will soon be here. My nest box for the screech owl has two inches of fresh wood shavings in it. There are two boxes set up in my scrub oak grove. The male will use one and keep watch over the female who will use the other. I have them placed so that he can see the entrance hole of his mate. Her box faces east so that she will have morning sun. He will receive the afternoon sun with his westerly facing roosting box. February is cold, yet there is a hint of warmer times not far off. Melting icicles hint of the spring thaw just around the corner. Black oil sunflower and Nyjer are favorites for the seed eaters. Suet provides energy for the insect-eating ruby-crowned kinglet that has remained in the backyard throughout the winter. Every once in a while I catch a glimpse of his neon red crown that he flashes. It is another hint that spring is not far away. Pheasant and quail march through the snow on my pathway to the ground feeders. The heated bird bath has lots of action throughout the day from birds who stop for a drink, as well as the robins and waxwings who bathe contentedly. March dawns and I hear the house finch singing as the morning sun warms the birds. His song signals that winter is loosening its grip and spring will soon prevail. Spring will bring the breeding season and new birds will soon arrive on their migration. Winter residents prepare to leave and the cycle begins anew.

Who needs a calendar to tell them what time of year it is? The natural rhythms and cycles let me know what time it is and what to expect next. I have reversed the convertible nest box so the chickadees will find it ready for their new nest. House wrens are singing. The flicker has started to drum on our wood-burning stove stack. The machine-gun staccato of his drumming wakes me this morning. My wife asks me, "Who is knocking at the door?" "Spring," I answer. "Spring is here."

Citizen Science Programs
The Cornell Lab of Ornithology and the National Audubon Society have a wonderful array of citizen science programs for the family or the individual bird lover. You can contact the Cornell Lab of Ornithology at www.birds.cornell.edu/. Here is a brief list of some of their programs:

- nest-box monitoring project
- informal science education
- continent-wide research
- proactive conservation

- information related to cavity-nesting birds
- online nest-box cam
- Project Classroom feeder watch

Contact the National Audubon Society at www.audubon.org. They have local regional chapters that you can consider joining. These chapters engage in a variety of local conservation projects that benefit birds and other wildlife. Audubon conducted the 107th Christmas Bird Count in 2007. These projects help scientists in learning about long-range trends in bird populations: whether they are shrinking, expanding, or remaining the same.

Birds are a key indicator species. They can act as an early warning system when something is wrong in our environment. Other birding and conservation groups that can provide additional information:

- The Nature Conservancy (www.nature.org) is a wonderful national organization that promotes conservation and saving habitat. It has nature trails and has protected key species around the country with its important work.
- The American Birding Association (www.americanbirding.org) is an organization for those who want to become more serious in their study of birds.
- The American Bird Conservancy (www.abcbirds.org) maintains a Bird Conservation Alliance that helps groups further their knowledge and conservation work with birds.

Black-chinned
Hummingbird
page 19

Ruby-throated
Hummingbird
page 21

American
Goldfinch
page 25

White-breasted
Nuthatch
page 27

Carolina
Chickadee
page 23

Chipping
Sparrow
page 31

Carolina Wren
page 29

House Finch
page 33

House
Sparrow
page 35

Downy
Woodpecker
page 37

Tufted
Titmouse
page 39

White-throated
Sparrow
page 41

Eastern
Bluebird
page 43

Brown-
headed
Cowbird
page 45

Great-crested
Flycatcher
page 47

Purple Martin
page 49

European
Starling
page 51

Northern
Cardinal
page 53

Red-bellied
Woodpecker
page 55

American
Robin
page 57

Northern Mockingbird
page 59

Blue Jay
page 61

Mourning Dove
page 63

Common Grackle
page 65

Northern Flicker (Yellow-shafted)
page 67

Backyard Birds across the country!

BACKYARD BIRDS OF **California**

BACKYARD BIRDS OF **Florida**

BACKYARD BIRDS OF **Illinois**

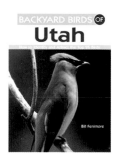

BACKYARD BIRDS OF **Utah**

BACKYARD BIRDS OF **Virginia**

Soon to include all 50 states.
Available in stores nationwide or directly from

Gibbs Smith, Publisher
1.800.835.4993/www.gibbs-smith.com